# Rhymes of Joy

*Preface by J.-K. Huysmans*

**Théodore Hannon**

Translated By Richard Robinson

Sunny Lou Publishing Company
Portland, Oregon, USA
http://www.sunnyloupublishing.com

Revised and Corrected: December 25, 2023
Original Publication Date: December 22, 2023

Translation Copyright © 2023 Richard Robinson.
All rights reserved.

ISBN: 978-1-955392-45-7

### #

This translation from French is based on the Gay et Doucé edition of *Rimes de joie*, Paris, 1881.

# Contents

Preface..................................................................5

Country Fair Incense ......................................17

Chinoiserie.........................................................21

Rough Weather..................................................23

Snows..................................................................24

Declaration.........................................................26

Opopanax............................................................27

Sky Sludge..........................................................31

Vow......................................................................32

The Good Corner...............................................33

Flowers of Fevers..............................................35

White Lilacs.......................................................36

In an Express Train...........................................37

Beloved Perfumes.............................................38

Offertory.............................................................41

Green Leaves.....................................................42

During the Grape Harvest...............................44

White Everywhere............................................45

Cyprien Tibaille.................................................47

| | |
|---|---|
| May Triolets | 50 |
| Good Gods | 52 |
| Drinkers of Phosphorus | 55 |
| Lemons | 60 |
| Seascapes | 61 |
| Skinniness | 63 |
| Grisaille | 67 |
| Jane's Fine Vices | 69 |
| A Genre Painting | 71 |
| Ex Voto | 73 |
| Byzantine Virgins | 74 |
| Absinthe Litanies | 77 |
| To Two Big Bizarre Eyes | 80 |
| Madrigal of Sorts | 82 |
| The Fur | 83 |
| Hymn | 84 |
| Make-up | 86 |

# Preface

Parnassianism, which was humiliated in or around the year of grace 1866 by that inexhaustible blather we call the Muse, was divided into two camps.

Poets in the one camp, including those who had newly hatched, were enamored with Leconte De Lisle and paraded before us, when it was their turn, an army of deeply moving puppets, old circus entertainers of Olympus, exhumed from the exhausting rhapsodies of Homer or the obscure mythologies of Finland or India.

Poets in the other camp, as followers of Victor Hugo, engaged in those corners of excessive sentimentalism and affectations of simplicity that the great master had redeemed, in days gone by, by the force of genius.

That they had dusted off all the religiosity of bygone times and, for the benefit of ideal dolls, sung plaintive romances is beside the point; the Parnassians obtained but one objective, the only objective they didn't pursue: boredom.

It is fitting however to recognize the service that they have rendered, and I point it out all the more willingly here because I feel in myself an old drop of tenderness for the clowns. If this school, – one of whose lesser masters, Théodore Banville, will doubtless remain one of its most contorted funambulists not to mention one of its most supple acrobats, – turned poetry into an exercise of gymnastics, a surprising jugglery of words, it will at least have freed us forever from those lamentable little grinding machines operated by men who, not knowing their profession, rhyme like ridiculous pedants! The misfortune was good for something. Like Romanticism, of which it is the last expression, Parnassianism had its purpose.

Now, if I except some artists who have never, for all that, belonged to Parnassianism, like Soulary or Sully-Prodhomme; if again I set aside, after the works of Auguste de Châtillon whose personality was distinct, the curious intimist poetry of Francois Coppée, nothing is left for me but to certify the utter discredit into which Parnassianism has fallen, the nothingness that it has produced.

Today it is dead. May the dirt that by bleeding irony a publisher causes to be shoveled onto the covers of its books by a naked and worn-out gravedigger, – be not too heavy for him!

I need not deal here with certain attempts that the last and least passionate Romantics have recently dared in modern times. Those works were stillborn, the last miscarriage of Romanticism. The stage is set then, and I expect that Naturalism, which although lacking a poem in verse has at least produced the most beautiful poem in prose that I know of, *l'Abbé Mouret*,[1] should do the same for the novel, – sweep

---

[1] *l'Abbé Mouret: La Faute de l'Abbé Mouret* by Émile Zola, published in 1875.

away all that hodgepodge of insanities and nonsense.

And that is really a disconcerting thing when you think about it. Waiting for a new poetic movement to have materialized, as it seemed it had to, that above all would not mix Goethe with Shakespeare, not pour Olivier Basselin in with Alfred de Musset, as M. Boucher did, not concoct for us, even while doling it out with true talent, mixtures of Villon, Chenier, Hugo, Châtillon, Vallès and Jules Choux, as M. Richepin did; it seemed finally that there was only one way for it to go, except of course while waiting for an even better movement to follow it, and nevertheless not one among the thousands of rhymers that fill up the displays with their works, to no benefit, had any doubts about it, not one of them placed a foot on the path blazed by the only modern master who was both alluring and curious, in spite of his exasperating devilment as a dandy and a romantic; by the only poet among them who had struck a really modern tone, who had, in those times of impassive and whimpering poetry, created a real and live work, who dared, in his day, to break the extolled molds created by Hugo; by the only poet among them who had resolutely embarked on a path, until then unexplored, of realism.

I am referring to the poet of genius who, like our great Flaubert, opens endless horizons with an adjective, the abstractor of the essence and of the subtlety of our debasements, the bard of those troubling hours when passion exhausts itself while seeking with impious attempts an appeasement of carnal madness; I am referring to the poet who rendered the immense void of simple loves, the implacable obsessive fears of the spleen, the rout of overworked senses, and the adorable grief of slow kisses that imbibe; the painter who initiated us into the melancholic charms of rainy seasons and ruined joys; I am referring to the prodigious artist who produced *The Flowers of Evil*, – Charles Baudelaire!

Well! A Belgian painter, M. Théodore Hannon, who, despite obsessive memories, shows himself in his *Rhymes of Joy* to be a singular and new poet, has boldly in certain poems of this book followed closely in the tracks of the great master. If he lacks his powerful allure, or his haughty griefs, or his profound ironies, he possesses at least the charming qualities of an advanced youth! If sometimes, primarily in his first book of poems, *Les vingt-quatre coups de sonnet*, he laments and cries over his infidelity; if like every young poet who respects himself, he celebrates the graces of his mistress and feels the need to curse her when she betrays him or leaves him, – he has nothing of that so very modern rancor born of boredom and disappointed expectation: being neither betrayed nor let go of. In the absence of such concentrated and plain verse, in the absence of the "meat" of Charles Baudelaire, he possesses exquisite mannerisms, sudden outbursts of minutely detailed and sustained joys, aspirations for Parisian elegances.

In this respect he belongs completely to the Naturalist school, but in terms of process, the manner of scrubbing his verse, the manner of engraving the stone and emphasizing the purity of the gold in the mountings, he takes more after the incomparable jeweler Théophile Gautier. Just like him, he has, in his good pieces, the word that makes an image, the unexpected and precise adjective that draws a picture from top to bottom and gives the scent of the thing he is charged with rendering; he has the right touch, the vibrant and glistening color.

His verse moves, flirts, pirouettes with strange tintinnabulations; sometimes it contorts, produces enjambments like that of the good Glatigny's verse, grazes *le concetti*, rises to the very surface, plants itself front and center and provokes, with affected dryness, mysterious and bizarre turns of phrase, in the manner of Tristan Corbière; it is covered in spangles, a combination of lamé and openwork, with a rose-colored tint in a totally Japanese style, with a truly charming fantasy of realism.

And then, in spite of the still-permitted use of Romantic verse that one could break in two without extracting even the least juice or marrow, M. Hannon produces, in a series of works under monotonous weather, a particular savor, a taste of Flemish soil, complicated by a very fine aroma of nervousness. There, that's the special note of this colorist, and it is finished off by an uneasy solicitude for those worldly refinements, for those feminine scents that enabled Émile Zola to write such beautiful, such admirable pages.

One of the few in fact among contemporary authors, M. Hannon has a curiosity for aggressive perfumes, disordered luxuries of undergarments and things that lie hidden, opulences of make-up in plain view. Beauties that dry at the end of stumps, or that liquify inside jars, enchant him.

He will certainly not be the poet who praises the bovine eyes of goddesses, those beads of water whence no sparkle gleams; he certainly won't be the poet who exalts statuesque or grave attitudes, the body's stiff fleshy parts caught glimpse of by outdated force of habit. To all these rolls of classic fabric, he prefers instead the undulations of silk and faille. He has understood the audacity or deceitfulness of the outfits of Rodrigue and Worth, the usefulness of fabrics that go against the milky grain of the flesh, the benefit of velvets that absorb the light or silks that reflect it, an accordance with the type of woman who wears them, complicated and studied jewelry, odors that agitate and sing quietly, all the spice that heats up this delicious bisque, the experimental charm of a Parisian.

But let's move on to the book itself and take, for starters, the most original piece, that which gives the timber of the poet: "Opopanax."

Divided into three parts, each of an unequal number of stanzas, Opopanax opens with a triumphant fanfare of horns, and little by little the entire orchestra flares up and sustains with a beautiful din of kettledrums and brass, the hymn that is unleashed, singing the libertine virtues of glorious perfume!

Then the symphony dies down, and as if the artist had sworn to render with the quill the different and nevertheless similar effects of poetry and painting, one those exquisite albums of Okou-Sai suddenly opens up before us, where, on the silky pulp of blond paper, a pink volcano, Mt. Fuji, tapers like an Adam's apple in a pale blue satin sky.

He makes us leaf through those marvelous watercolors where corn- and straw-colored harbors gently rock, on the ripple of their waters, the rainbow-colored crescents of junks; he makes us see in the pearl-grey smoke of twilight the assumption of a red moon grazed by white storks in flight; he makes stretch out before us boundless rice fields that the wind rolls through, those large rivers that seem to draw with them the purple of the hills that they reflect, upside down; then after a few more pages, he shows us, at their washstands, standing out from crimson tufts of giant peonies, the young courtesans of Edo, in their tight-fitting weaves of pale silk and silver blossoms, who part their lips with an enigmatic smile splashed with lacquer and glazed with golden dots.

The album has closed. Another opens, an album of impressionistic painting, where the pages follow one after the other, exhaling this imperiously urgent smell of modernity found in Degas, Manet, Rops. I don't know anyone presently among the poets with the strength to produce a similar piece of work, with its rendering of subtle ideas and its battle waged against the inexpressible.

Other pieces follow, exhibiting a really cheerful malady, among which "Make-up", that extraordinary hosannah celebrating the mournful charm of withered epidermis. Like Baudelaire, in his superb study of Constantin Guys, the artist exults before the paste and sauce of make-up, and it must be seen with what delicateness of touch, with what lightness of hand, with what salutary caress and what gentle touch of the spangling skin, hovering just at the surface, he pastels and recasts, only to remove it all again with his kisses – the face of his mistress whom he abandons himself to making love to!

I have to mention a number of other poems: "Skinniness," where the infantile attractions of skinny beauties appear in the light of apotheosis; an original "Offertory"; a sonnet entitled "Flowers of Fevers" which deals with a troubling depravity; another placed under the title of "Rough Weather"; then "Jane's Fine Vices"; "Drinkers of Phosphorus"; "Byzantine Virgins," treating of suspect madonnas who stand up at the bottom of banal iconostases with their stockings embossed with gold coins, their blushed cheeks, their watery eyes, their bleeding lips, mechanically licked by the tip of their tongue; "The Fur," one of the most nicely polished pieces in the book; and, finally, like a good kiss, "Country Fair Incense," a beautiful description of a Flemish Kermess, painted with broad strokes and full of those exquisite mannerisms that are, as I mentioned earlier, one of the distinctive marks of the poet.

In summary, notwithstanding several jolts in its rhymes and a few twisted phrases, this volume is, while anticipating even greater realistic works, stronger works, works that have a procedure that I'm still not quite aware of, one of the most interesting collections of verse that has appeared in recent years. All said, it is, since Baudelaire, and after Glatigny's *Antres malsains* and certain other pieces of his, the only one that has bound itself to the unhealthy charms of the female sex, to the elegant neuroses of large cities.

In this way, *Rhymes of Joy*, like an amusing fantasy, joins the ranks of the great movement of Naturalism.

– J.-K. HUYSMANS
Paris, August, 1879.

# Rhymes of Joy

*1876-1881*

# Country Fair Incense

Dear, remember the heavy, country fair bouquet
That the sovereign people greedily inhaled.
The fifes poured out their vinegar into the night.
The bugle sneezed into the face of the brass and
Out-of-tune valve horns. In discordant beat,
    The meager drums boomed.

But even more stridently into the air was dispelled
A gamut of odors to defy every sense of smell,
And more fiercely broke out the fanfare
Of frying oils and acrid lard,
Unleashing their intense stench through the sweet air
    Where your flared nostrils grow alarmed.

Scrupulous *journaliste*, I noted, without rancor,
The curious voices and cries of that choir,
Whose sweet-smelling harmony penetrated my nose:
White pudding, mussels dressed in black, purple-
      jacket crabs,
Golden potatoes, violet sausages,
    O sizzling symphony!

When the white and green tram stopped, I held out
My hand to you. Your leg flashed: you descended.
The ground guarded the exquisite toes of your *mules*.[2]
Suddenly an enormous gust of smells
Rose up from a whirlwind of flames and moistures
    In good old Flemish fashion.

---

[2]*mule* – a backless shoe, similar to a clog, but more elegant. From Latin *mulleus calceus*, red shoe.

At first it was the sickly exhalation of tallow
Rising to heaven in convulsive spasms.
On large stoves the fritters hissed:
Grease in slow swirls rotates the blond prisms
That turn, come, go, mount, foul-smelling,
    Plunge and make flourishes.

Beside a redhead with vulgar cuffs,
In skirts starched by burnt fat, the fritters
Mushroomed, powdered with pale brown sugar,
O swellings of undigested dough! Their tears
Congealed at length in floral crockery,
    And reeked to high heaven.

Waffles smelling suspiciously of grilled bread
Made a pyramid with their squared domes
Where the sugar had left a point of frost.
Mushy gingerbread loaves mixed their flat odor
With cakes displaying their shiny roundness,
    Like brass medals.

Mussels on the fire groaned piteously.
Then their shells, like the beaks of greedy birds,
Opened; and all around, the marine effluvia
Took you by the throat, evoking an unknown sea
Where some bitter wrack rotted,
    Most dreadful for nostrils.

In the shade, – your nose shuddered then with great
    disdain!
Puddings browned in smoky casseroles,
Sometimes a fried onion joined its confident notes

To the choir of sausages that burst out in the night:
The flames burst their belly with a very sharp
   And spattering noise.

Farther away, lying flat in wide wicker baskets,
Suffocating *schols*[3] opened their gullets
And, shamelessly, displaying the lilies of unwell
       flesh,
Arched their back when slit into strips for a penny.
Infections around which the rogue
   With covetous looks walks back and forth.

Next it was, ambulant asphyxia! the rich
And burlesque baskets that marched past us in the
       arms
Of some frightening old woman with a raspy voice,
Baskets that effused their scented bouquet:
Shrimp, snails, hardboiled eggs, cheval fumé,
   Whereby you were seized with bouts of nausea!

The horror of Chinese lanterns with their gloomy
       glow
Floated over a sea of sweaty blouses;
Shipwreck: in a corner a harpist droned.
Sometimes a beauty cut her way through the rough
       crowd;
Above her very high heels the essence of patchouli
   Lingered, betraying her passage.

At disdainful angles she puckered her lips
And her nose quivered with superb disgust,
While around us in warm turbulences,

---

[3]*schols*: a Dutch word for European plaice, a kind of flounder.

Nonstop, and towards dark skies, the smell of
 salted fish mounted
And lards clarioned, dense exhalations
 Of nutritious stenches!

All the while as the country fair lit its incenses,
Me, I walked blissfully at your side, my senses
Ravished by the spring odor that hovers
About your skin, – unmindful of the garlic wafts
That your large fan, saturated with *frangipane*,
 Stirred up in its flutterings.

# Chinoiserie

I have on my table a Chinese vase,
Of finest taste, that many a man
Would contemplate, forever on end
With the ecstasy of a fetish.

The sun cherishes its pale lip,
For in its lactescent enamel
Ever a caressing ray of light
Sets some opal gem on it.

On its bluish, polished sides
Begins to unfold a stunning flora,
Of ineffable beauty,
That a strange caprice adorns.

The eye discovers among the flowers
That encrimson its blue banks,
Monsters espied in dreams:
Haggard dragons, mocking sphinxes,

Crazy chimeras, gauche birds,
And bizarre Barbary apes,
Cool witnesses to those cinnabar
And indigo debaucheries.

Japan! Pink Promised Land!
Resonating with the crystalline chant
Of kaolin turrets
That a fairyland river wets!

Soothed by scents of tea
In the oblivion that great alders cast,
I long in this new Lethe
For the junk of yellow mandarins.

Yes, in this marvelous sojourn
I would live, deaf fate willing,
At the foot of a Chinese olive
Hopped up on opium and love.

# Rough Weather

Lugubrious weather! Gloomy sky with a hateful brow
Where an accursed cloud with heavy flanks gallops
And batters the sinister sea, flies into a rage, bursts,
Then blends its waves with the waves of the deaf
        flood.

No laughter, no rays: the beaches are deserted.
Already the shivering swarm of bathers flee,
And the forlorn sand is marked with green algae
Where soft-sounding women's heels once gleamed.

The sea roars with great wrath, bellows, rears up,
Inviting to a macabre waltz the black waves
That gulls' wings lash while in flight.

Far away, beyond the surge with troubling cries,
As from within my heart where a deaf tear wells,
Some alarum cannon rumbles, vaguely.

      – Nieuport-Bains.

# Snows

Under your Havana-brown or green hat, –
Grebe's belly or Lophophorus', –
Your gleaming eyes of phosphorus
Sparkled, completely wide open.

At first, among the arabesques that rime
Engraved on a dull pane of glass,
Your pupil, intoxicating to my melancholy,
Walked, sending shivers down my spine.

Then your fingernail, my sweetheart,
All trembling, severed from a heart
The flora whose branches mocking winter
Traced on my silvered window pane.

After your painful departure,
It is through this symbolic strait,
O female magician,
That my melancholic gaze slipped.

Snow everywhere in the distance!
The plain, covered to the horizon,
White under its brilliant *barège*[4],
Spreads its large frozen face.

Yonder, a freshly powdered hill
Terminates the skies' white wadding.
Everywhere the scintillating ermine
Monotonously stretches before my eyes...

---

[4]barège: (textile) a fabric of light wool from Barèges.

Under an inexorable avalanche
Nothing but one gamut and one ray:
Against the inflexible white hue,
Who dares to try his drawing pencil?

But, suddenly from this plaster sky,
A dark raven whose branchy foot
Scatters stars of alabaster
Fell like a drop of black ink.

And I thought I saw, as if in a dream,
A dot of ebony in that milk-white wave,
His snow-covered breast where a grain of beauty
Sparkled relentlessly.

# Declaration

The great name of spouse should not bind us;
I do not want to be your lover, Madam,
Your King Charlie, nor your chandler,

Even less can I be your brother – not a chance!

I have no desire to be the servant,
The fan carrier or umbrella carrier,
Some dear cousin, or the follower,

The Lord Protector, the friend you scold...

No, bound to you only by one of those hairs
That veil your intensely fierce eyes,
I want, O modest desire! I want to be

The page who places your beauty marks.

# Opopanax

I

Opopanax! a very bizarre name,
And a perfume that is even bizarrer!
Opopanax, the sound of the horn
Is faint compared to your fanfare!

A bouquet of roses, blandness!
And blandness is the ocean's breath,
When you charm my nose,
Strange lullaby, O what strong odor!

In your shocking syllables
Fumes an unfamiliar incense,
Its caresses evoke on our senses
A vision of gallant nights:

Naked torsos, sweaty necks,
Hair let down and scented
By your abracadabra aroma,
Snow-white flesh tones, warm glimmers.

The lily is yellow compared to your arms
And spiritless is the coiling of snakes,
Interlacing in ardent harmonies:
A virgin's tears, a faun's rictus!

Amber, patchouli, musk
Enjoy, compared to your red breath,
A brief stench that the servant

Uses to scent her busk.[5]

## II

You hail from a land of oriental vases,
Where stunning butterflies
Constellate the vermillion skies,
Skies adorably counterfeit!

You perfume those marvelous
Edens of faience and lacquer
Where the storks' beak clacks on
Green, yellow, and blue domes.

To your impure blood, to your tears,
Chaste myrrh says: "*RACA!*"
*Opopanax pastinaca*,
Flora with a rackety name.

Along the golden plains of rice
Your breath runs, your perfume roams,
Musking the mauve lakes embroidered
By the purple flowering pear trees.

A Chinese woman, with bronze glows,
Applies it to her golden fingernails
And her citron-colored throat where doze
The insane desire of bonzes[6].

A Japanese woman in her ransoms

---

[5]busk: baleen, or corset. From French "busc."

[6]bonzes: Buddhist priests.

Employs your acrid spittle
To enhance her olive-colored skin,
To ensorcel her love hickies.

### III

O MARION, you, a Japanese lady
With your imperceptible feet,
These scents are the familiar scents
Of your budding body that I kiss.

Body of a secret pagan art,
Marble made flesh, sea foam,
Fruit pulp, pigment, blonde flower,
A woman's skin and the skin of a baby!

From the tobacco-brown frizz
On the nape of your neck, sun rays,
Down to the clouds of your big toe,
This vanquishing balm struts.

Rolling down the slope of your breasts,
It runs along your arms, strolls
Over your red lips, and volplanes
Above your great provocative kisses.

It haunts this long rose-colored *peignoir,*
This peignoir of living tissue,
That my kisses often embrace
And sometimes my tears moisten.

It embeds its teasing spirit
Into your furbelows, O mistress,

From the velvet of your braids
To the knots of your brodequins.

It swims around your naked skin
And seems your flesh's incense,
Which, fully troubled, fills the air
With an unfamiliar drowsiness.

\* \* \* \* \* \* \* \* \* \* \* \* \* \* \*
\* \* \* \* \* \* \* \* \* \* \* \* \* \* \*
\* \* \* \* \* \* \* \* \* \* \* \* \* \* \*
\* \* \* \* \* \* \* \* \* \* \* \* \* \*

I cannot tell on these nights of verve
When you bite me black and blue,
Whether it is this impudent poison
Or your saliva that most unnerves me.

No matter! provided, to get intoxicated,
While your gorgeous body straddles the couch,
You pour for me with open mouth
The Opopanax of your kisses!

# Sky Sludge

The pendulum whispers with mocking laughter.
On my panes the rain in sad drops clacks
And finds many a sympathetic echo in my heart.
The faraway sky has the opacity of lacquer.

On my panes the rain in sad drops clacks.
With caressing blows the storm is victor.
The faraway sky has the opacity of lacquer:
The day is gray, still grayer is my rancor.

With caressing blows the storm is victor.
The dull sky's reflection saddens many a puddle.
The day is gray, still grayer is my rancor.
A tenacious spleen clings to everything and clutches.

The lifeless sky's reflection saddens many a puddle.
Spleen everywhere grips us like a hardened tracker:
A tenacious spleen clings to everything and clutches...
Beneath dark skies our mourning seems brighter, O
       my heart!

# Vow

From your cup I drank, my love,
The wine of huge voluptuousnesses.

On your body whiter than day
I culled the flower of insanities.

From your mouth of mauve desires
I gathered the nectar of strange juices,

The sweet torments and pleasures
That were my mad grape harvests.

My lips, from your swoons,
Tasted enchanting tears;

Your heart, rich in subtle poisons,
Poured for me new drunkenesses.

From your eyes filled with heavy sleep
Descend my sick gaieties:

Tomorrow my heart, under the glances,
Can hang from your vermillion fingertips...

But, so as not to die a coward,
I want, and before I am skinned alive,

To bite the carnal peaches of sin
Growing from your immaculate espalier!
.

# The Good Corner

The half-open cave is dark.
A spider spins its web there,
Or else it makes a swing
At the end of a falling string.

The antique plaster crumbles;
The traveling slug in lime
Draws arabesques on the wall
With its silver slime.

The door is well-bolted
That protects this hideout,
A hallway dear to woodlice
Leads there by zigzags.

Wrapped in a venerable hay,
The wine of respectable forebears
Sleeps an admirable slumber
That goes back one century – or two!

It is health, it is joy, that
These stoppered bottles harbor,
Whose glaucous sides glimmer
Under dusty flakes.

One keeps for many a somber evening
These great wines pouring steady,
For at the bottom of the glasses melancholy
With its leaden mask vanishes.

There and then, in the enchanting room,
With a soul crazy about wine bottles, –
What a mouth-watering battle!
To be bombarded with corks

And pummeled with glassfuls of wine,
Enough to fill a well,
To see all one's sullen cares unwind
And fly away, and then

To taste, – face flat on the table
And buried in shadows, –
The delectable victory,
The victory of forgetfulness!

# Flowers of Fevers

Paris, city where the flesh in full bloom blossoms,
Paris overflows in provocative bosoms
And, like a espalier glorious in hanging fruit,
Proudly bulges with its large breasts of a bacchante.

The corset sags and cracks under a load of flesh
But, busk-enabled, tautens toward twin points.
Shamelessly you powder the two ardent mounts,
A corsage dearly prized by Jordaens,[7] doubtless.

Around me, affectionate, in foaming frothing swells,
This novel ocean overwhelms me, intoxicates me;
Its all-white wave trying to wage an assault on me...

But I like pale and lanky girls, flowers of fevers!
For I want to stroll my fingernails and lips over
The bodies of those virgins with their boyish
      skinniness.

    – Paris.

---

[7] Jordaens: Jacob Jordaens, the seventeenth-century Flemish painter.

# White Lilacs[8]

*For Louise Abbéma.*

Provocative – and Parisian,
To the very tips of her eye lashes,
She has large eyes, mischievous and subtle,
That peer into the distance, overheated *da Siena.*

She emerges from the golden frame,
The lively flower of bitumen!
A blonde florescence scented with
Moos-Rose or Cosmydor.

In Veronese-green satin
Her childish grace grows turbulent,
A child whose triumphant appeal
Would enslave the *Farnese Hercule.*

Her frail wrists, never tiring,
And her slender, long-gloved hands
Sparkle with silver flowers
From a bouquet of pale lilacs.

In her, all is feverish and joy!
Her silly simpers beam and
Vanquish dark December days:
She is April in a silken frock.

---

[8]Original footnote: Paris Salon, 1878.

# In an Express Train

The machine all of a sudden belches soot,
Cracks the air with brass screeches and departs in a
    hullabaloo.
Everything trembles... Hup! It muddles in one
    devouring pace
Meadows and fields and woods, where Dawn wipes
    away the tears.

At river banks the steam stitches together blonde
    clouds.
Hup! hup! Inert locomotive!... I make myself hoarse.
Hurry up! Faster! What are afraid of?... Every wheel
    turn
Brings me closer to you, and shortens the roads.

The telegraph wires extend their reach
Where the fledgling, a black note, practices scales
Which the North Wind modulates in hurried gales.

The whistle moaned. The train stops. – At last
In my heart the hour of heated passions tintinnabulate
And I fly, this sonnet on your lips to consummate!

# Beloved Perfumes

I

When at night, like a thief,
Deserting the enervating alcove,
I free myself from your proud arms,
Feeling weak, voiceless, and cold.

When, hastening through the cold streets
With bloodshot eye and pale visage,
I regain, feverish and with a stiff step,
Sadly my sad abode.

When, severing the mournful shadows
With an indecisive pace, and overcome with emotion,
I reflect, quietly within myself...
The horror of midnights englooms me.

Muffled in this mantle of shadows
Favorable to reveries,
I shuffle along, savoring the gateau
Of cherished memories.

Not bothered by the evening vagabonds
Gazing at me with a strange look,
Not seeing the brute who, brushing by me,
Stumbles in the gutter for booze,

Not seeing the girl who jiggles
In the cadences of a satin dress,
Not answering the sad call of trollops

With a smile painted on their face.

Protected by your image
(It is such a tutelary image!)
I escape, the memory of you heavy
On my skin – like a scapular.

    II

Over the roofs the wind rages,
Lamentable; the weather vane
Grows possessed, grates, pirouettes
Under a dark sky that rains.

In penitential garment,
The moon beams with malicious intent.
I don't give a hoot! I'm moving, I'm moving,
With doleful nerves, the flesh content.

Your strong and pungent aroma
Still lingers in my hair,
The soul of your caresses slumbers
On my lips, on my cheeks.

At night, in the middle of the fog,
Your bouquet expands with every step,
And the subodorant chorus of your flesh
Follows me, petal and pulp.

A chorus that intoxicates and protects me
With all its scented soul! –
Wrapped in your perfumes, gentle *cortege*,
I advance, with eyes closed,

And under an ink-black sky I still imagine
Myself snuggled up in your hair,
In the hollow of your breasts, the adorable harbor
Where my desires have dropped anchor.

# Offertory

It was night. In full mourning the sea celebrated
The death of day. A chorus of frigid darkness
Fell from a sad black sky that was brightened

By stars, the steel nails of those funerary vaults.

A dismal wind bowed down the swollen waves in the
        distance;
The ocean whimpered mortuary hymns
Like a giant organ groaning a slow *De Profundis,*

And the sound seemed to stir the winding sheets...

The moon, triumphant and round, suddenly burned
With its disk floating over an uncertain sea
While a funerary gaggle of large osprey

With drawn-out cries approached to kiss the paten.

# Green Leaves

As in my heart that goes forth singing,
As in my flesh filled with wonder,
May smiles in the meadows, radiant,
And the forest has awakened.

How I love the scent of the woods,
That perfumer of breezes!
I imbibe it through all my pores,
My dream feeds on it and grows tipsy.

The morning dew in globules
Iridesces at the tip of grass blades;
In the moss, like flowering velvet,
The muguet tintinnabulates.

Through the feverish meanders
Of both forest and plain,
The dragonfly and geometrid
Fondle each other, enamored.

Deep within green foliage,
Two birds spoon; the female, white-hot,
Employs her wings like two fans
To cool herself as she swoons.

Emotional, I flee through the shady arches
Where a blackbird whistles at me,
That master Scapin[9] of birds!
My feet grow moist in the wet grass.

---

[9]Scapin: a stock character from the *commedia dell'arte*.

I am blinded by the greenery.
The leaf implacably glitters.
And the blackbird mockingly trills at me:
*"Come back and see it from behind!"*

# During the Grape Harvest

Toward the sky glowing red with evening's rouge,
A vermillion slope of vineyards climbs:
The incarnadine of grapes enhances
The sanguine[10] that October paints with red-stained hands.

The female grape-harvesters climb, pink among the russet colors,
In short skirts, sounding a scarlet fanfare.
Their mouths, sanguine flowers, are soft and alert
While the purple vinestock is aroused by their fingers.

The haughty coquelicot that nights will fade,
Forgotten by autumn in these ardent expanses,
Is a garnet ablaze with the grape clusters' warm rubies.

Wine reddens their arms, but redder still are their faces,
When among their branches you number, O son of France,
Passions that make your madder pants pale.

— Nancy.

---

[10]sanguine: a red chalk drawing.

# White Everywhere

    Now, Winter, that distinguished perfumer
With his tuft of swan feathers,
    Spreads his violet fingers.
Snow stitches the hems of rooves.

    With a powered wig on,
And curled up in a shawl
    Made of the brightest cotton flocs,
The countryside takes on grand airs.

    The black crow turns ecstatic
For the revelry of white – milk of Tonka,
    Cream of Asia! – into which
He dips his bloody rostrum.

    The city radiates in its wedding dress,
Freshly starched.
    Wreaths of orange blossoms
Are seen snowing on its head.

    What whiteness in the street
Where the gruff *bise* grates!
    Trembling, I fly towards you,
Towards your small bedroom where all is white:

    Your wall hangings and your drapes,
Your very low furniture, your girdles,
    The bed where my face turns pale,
Your dressing gowns and the bed canopy,

      And your body, which terrifies me,
Icy flesh, living snow,
      Which my kisses with their fire
Forever try to warm, vainly.

# Cyprien Tibaille[11]

> "He wanted to turn his great sadness into a foil for joy. He would have wanted to embrace a woman flamboyantly dressed like an acrobat, in winter, under a yellow and gray sky, a sky that was about to snow, in a room hung with fabric wall hangings made in Japan, while some scraggy bloke emptied a barrel organ of sad waltzes that its belly was full of." – *The Vatard Sisters.* J.-K. Huysmans

In the accouterment of a maiden,
That pride of fairground entertainments,
You made your waist's movements
Complement the swelling of your bosom.

A line of bister was darkening
Your eyes with a strange shadow,
And on your brow an orange powder
Like a setting sun was applied.

O peerless saltimbanque,
With gold in the brodequins,
And on your chignon enough sequins
To break the bank.

In the ravine of your chest,
From Kananga,[12] ever in celebration,
Unwholesome blasts made a racket
To rout my senses.

It is in this way that my artist's spleen

---

[11]Cyprien Tibaille: a character in two of Huysmans' earlier novels, *Les Sœurs Vatard* (1878) and *En ménage* (1881).

[12]Kananga: capital city of the erstwhile Belgian Congo.

And my bizarre passion
Desire to possess you
Under a serene and sad winter sky,

An ochre and grey-striped sky,
Whence the obsessed snow will fall...
Your bedroom would be decorated
From cyma to wainscoting

With elegant Chinese fabrics
And panels wherein Japan
Brocades the weft of the crepe[13]
With extravagant flowerings.

Along unknown rivers,
Chimeras and hippogryphs
Eye us, raising their claws
Above bizarre horizons.

But in the discreet penumbra
A moon that Edo polishes
Would grow full on the bed's canopy,
A witness to our innumerable kisses.

. . . . . . . . . . .

Meanwhile, louder than our grunts,
Than our sighs or than the cries
Of our two aching hearts,
A tune with sepulchral notes

Below the windows groaned.

---

[13] crepe – the fabric (not the foodstuff).

The music is dismaying,
At first alive, then dying:
Atrocious organ, – but also friendly!

You grumble, you cry, you jeer.
Your song, lamentable plaything,
Makes the thin mahogany quiver
When you blare your entrails.

Mine are the laugh and the hiccough,
And the sobs and the voices critical
Of those grand tunes that you massacre,
Automatic parrot!

Come quell with the ravished clamors
Of your ever energetic throat
The cries of my restless nerves
And my unappeased hungers!

# May Triolets

At the back of parks, chestnut trees
Have set afire their girandoles;
Trembling with spring breezes
At the back of parks, chestnut trees
Hide spring loves
Performing tender Farandoles.
At the back of parks, chestnut trees
Have set afire their girandoles.

Come into the murmuring forest
To rekindle ancient kisses.
In dark copses, the blackberry flourishes;
Come into the murmuring forest
Under the complaisant foliage,
Near the birds that are musicians...
Come into the murmuring forest
To rekindle ancient kisses.

Rolling in the grass, let's make
Flowering cherry trees blush!
The sun shines on magnificent meadows;
Rolling in the grass, let's make
Bright bouquets from plain sprays,
For your bosom, those pretty praters.
Rolling in the grass, let's make
Flowering cherry trees blush!

Let's go, O my mad companion,
Let's lead our affections onto the green.
Through the heady countryside,

Let's go, O my mad companion:
Spring, much more than champagne,
Will intoxicate our reawakened hearts.
Let's go, O my mad companion,
Let's bring our affections onto the green!

# Good Gods

*For Ludwig Wihl.*

I

Brahma, Zarame, Orsi, Jehovah, Jupiter
    Thor with the burgrave's beard,
Zeus, Allah, Vishnu, God, – *filius et pater*,
    A matter of serious interrogation.
Cruel tyrants cast in gold or bronze,
    Made of wood, sculpted in stone,
Idols with hard hearts and uncalm expressions,
    Monsters with stiff eyelids,
You all have hands red with blood,
    Red human blood that steams!
To gain your love, all-powerful, it appears that
    The altar must reek
With the crimson liquor of savage stench;
    Cruel wild beasts, you want
The vein opened and hearts gasping for breath,
    To dip your ferocious claws into.
O! all this spilled blood must go somewhere,
    An ocean of somber setting
Greater than you, O Gods! where, for your twilight,
    A tenebrous squadron lies in wait...
But their terrible hand that wanted to crush us
    Shall reach out toward us, in vain,
When these hangmen shall drown in your midst,
    A bottomless sea stretched out before them!
We will let the Gods pass away one by one...
    In the empty and taciturn heaven,
One day we will burn strong-smelling sugar:

Time has quite gnawed away at Saturn!

II

O you, universal legatee of the Gods
    Who have disappeared, God the Father,
Be on your guard, really! Your priests are odious,
    Their hypocrisy exasperates.
They have none of the beauty of Old Testament sacrificers,
    Nor the haughtiness of Druids:
Our blood can sleep in our veins, these spoilers
    Want less fluid gifts!
Their weapon is the impudent bowl of mendicants
    Who beg along the highways.
They are extremely dull; their long, coarse, claw-like fingers
    Search for gold and leave breadcrumbs.
Beware! Your heaven cracks and the tarnished azure
    Shows fissures everywhere.
Your bell tolls. Your infiniteness is finite.
    Relegated to attics they will be,
Pale divinity, your glory, and your figureheads,
    Fate, Chance, Providence, Destiny!
These days our minds, quite emancipated,
    Have won their independence.
Your infantile hell, your Devil and his terrors,
    Everyone is overjoyed by them in all honesty,
For to untangle your rosary of errors
    We interrogate Science.
Your cult has the bitter sadness of hospices,
    With their fastings and hair shirts;
But we have introduced the deadly Sins

      To inexhaustible delights.
On our heads you can brandish your lightning,
      The whip you use to repay us, –
Here's a fig for your thunder! A fig for its blinding light:
      For we have forged the lightning rod!

# Drinkers of Phosphorus[14]

I

I despise these worn out girls,
Whoring about in the evening,
Selling themselves for anisettes,
Speaking shrill, drinking sweet.

Yes, I abhor these horrible urchins,
With unwholesome youthful instincts.
I abhor their gestures, their expressions,
Already perverse at sixteen!

Precocious flowers of a simple vice,
Wilting in one night,
What's to be gleaned from these husks,
Their corsets, where boredom haunts?

They have flat chests,
With no thrill in the foreplay, –
Can one really love these planks?
They make one hate skinniness.

But there is no public celebration
Where these puerile beauties,
Amidst shocked crowds,
Don't sport their stupid gaieties.

Revelers at night in their dresses,

---

[14]Phosphorus: By poetic license and analogy, loose women. A reference also to absinthe.

By day, working to feed their bellies;
Some are honest linen maids,
Others are laundresses of fine clothing.

Over here, sewers of boots,
Over there, seamstresses of gloves,
And others, libertinesses, tailor
The shirts of elegant people.

Their roost? A vague garret
Where a musky smell of ill repute lingers.
At the head of a hard, shiny bed,
Some Virgin or some patron Saint.

When their luck runs out,
They marry a cuckold who,
Loveless and sexless, deals them
More blows than sweet coo-coos!

With them, the smallest thing brings out
A temperamental fit:
Without passion and without excuse,
They fly stupidly into a rage.

A love affair is a stroll in the park.
A man for them is merely an arm
To escort them to *brasseries*,
To install them in the Alhambras.

Not thirsty – similar to how they caress –
They drink like bottomless wells.
Their brains are ever flaccid:
They make no sound, no *froufrous*

And keep under wraps, intact,
On jaunts, their feeble reasoning.
O what hopeless dolls,
With bellies full of gas!

They have no desire, no dreams,
No intelligent laughter, no tears:
These pitiful daughters of Eve
Have bitten the apple in the bud.

II

Artists, my brothers, poets,
Let us idealize our pleasures,
By never casting before swine
Our insatiable desires!

The mind makes vice flourish,
We must escape banality:
Would that the mistress might ravish us
Much by her strangeness!

It is from these bizarre women…
In their frightful arsenals
That rare arms glisten
Tempered by fierce furnaces.

Their sharp gaze is a broadsword
Piercing you to the marrow,
From their hair emanates
A strong and savage scent.

Their caresses open wounds
That bleed your soul at length,
And their kisses are bites,
Their big, loud kisses!

Over their flesh of sinewy form
Hovers a strong and subtle odor.
More effectively than chloroform
It drugs you, it puts you to sleep,

It rocks you with the cadences
Of irresistible languor... –
But, O what wild confidences
Whispered from heart to heart,

When a bewitching coquetry
Bites them, stoking to a pitch,
To the point of hysteria, –
The ritornello of a kiss!...

They need love on their own terms,
Love demanding nourishment!
Their bed is a battlefield:
You must conquer there or die.

Back off, grumpy virtues,
Simpering and convictionless!
Get up, naughty slatterns,
Go powder your noses.

With shoulder-length hair,
Our cuirass is without defect.
We are not eunuchs, by God.

These are the women we need!

Let's love these women, poets!
At their feet, let us spread out our swards:
We will see germinating in our heads
Sonnets with hot odors,

Stanzas with winged rhymes,
Verses strong and gleaming!
Let us love them zealously, painters:
They know how to revive our Art

And Pride with boisterous voices,
At the bottom of desperate hearts,
And in the somnambulant neurons
Of dephosphorated cerebellums!

# Lemons

*For Jules Clare.*

The stall gleamed with the morning's flames.
Overheated mullet reflected their cinnabar
On the bellies of turbot in satin robes,
And silver salmon had the shine of sabers.

On milky marble tiles pug cod lay,
Weighty neighbors to the iridescent bleak;
In their purple jerkins lobsters shined brilliantly
Near algae where verdigris oysters gaped.

But most of all the lemons charmed me: joyous fruit
Puncturing like a firm breast their fine silky paper...
Their scent is sweeter to me than the scent of
      strawberries.

And long would I enjoy their seductive contours;
For standing before the basket of shiny, tapering
      lemons,
I dream of Japanese women's pale golden nipples.

# Seascapes

### I

*The Bathing Hour*

On the wet sand the large heavy wheel creaks. Hup!
Hup! The bathing machine is at the water's edge.
Thin arms, brown round necks glisten in the rays that
    tattoo.

And the hot sun bites bare arms and amber necks!

The torso arches and cracks in the shuddering bathing
    suit,
The North Wind blows and molds to its bold designs
The luminous contour that is disimprisoned...

And the immodest breeze applies kisses...

Fastening collars to disdainful necks,
The laughing wave whips and beats the supple sides,
Despite your mannered cries, O craven bathers...

And the lascivious surge embraces the white bodies.

### II

*The Upset Sea*

The sea gapes. Its waves, irritated, enrage.
The swell foams and hisses, throwing into the air,

Like a long crack of the whip, its stormy mane,

A monstrous whip taken for a flash of lightning.

The sea is, this morning, quite dark, quite austere.
It emits strange voices and fantastic cries
That, trembling, gainsay the earth, her ancient sister;

And the echoes from afar hurl, afflicted...

Now, before this sea with its fierce fanfares,
I think of your eyes, remarkable, black and profound,
And terrible like hers: your large and bizarre eyes

That hold me drowned in bottomless sounds.

# Skinniness

I

I love your glabrous body,
That frail body of a boy,
Supple, svelter than a grass-blade,
And seductive like a sonnet.

I love those straight, male lines
That hug you tightly, rigidly
In their skinniness, wherein you caress
My painter's and lover's eye.

You took these hard-lined limbs
From some Florentine bronze;
I find in them a crafty grace
That struggles with an infantile charm.

Your ephebic body, O real woman,
Drives all my troubled senses crazy
With its allures of ryegrass
Sown by the wind in a wheat field.

It has the attraction and
The disquieting grip of serpents,
Always some red imprint
Persists of its spruce embrace.

I love its osteology
Bolstered by nerves of steel
And muscles whose energy

Would make a carnivore envious!

The enticing skinniness of your bust
Which seems like a child's...
Or like a reed, nimble and robust,
Stands up triumphant;

It arches out at the clavicles,
And its bosom has for fleurons
Two pointed breasts, – minuscule
Like the tips of lemons!

## II

All my naughty-themed dreams
Incline towards you, O my tomboy,
For the pupils of your eyes nonplus
The most orthodox of projects.

If by necessity, my fool, my sage,
A new Adam were damned,
The old Serpent in your corsage
Would cull the forbidden fruit!

The flame of great vice shines
In your long undisciplined eyes,
And, to please me, the seven sins,
Have deeply rooted in you.

Among the Greeks, your unusual shape,
Would have tempted many a proud sculptor,
A pagan body that the *Hermaphrodite*
Would have chosen for a brother, – or sister!

### III

Fie on the heavy and spineless fat
With its invading sediments!
Fie on the fat! the prude
Stifles your bold contours.

It would blunt all your edges,
The honor of your much celebrated body,
The skinniness wherein you cinch,
Picturesquely, your beauty.

The overflowing and rebel wave
Would level your precious hollows
With kisses that their procession
Planted on your flesh.

Your lines, hard and masterful
In their powerful neuropathy,
Under the bloating of fat
Would stump their rude accent.

Then what pillage of masterpieces!
Your great arms, with the soft and tenacious
Entwinement of a garden snake,
Would thicken in a bourgeois fashion.

Your muscular and straight leg
Like a superb culm, alas!
Would wear down your narrow *mule*
And your cream stocking with lilac edges.

Finally, on your virile hips,
Your breast with a virginal seal
And your chest, ideal plank,
Would swell up in banal bosom.

## IV

Keep, forever keep, O dream!
Your troubling plasticity,
Your svelteness, your brief form,
Your nerves, your masculinity,

Your imperceptible ankles
And your minuscule wrists
Your irresistible shoulders
Where my teeth leave their imprint.

Your skillful hands, armed with nails
That tear, quite sharply,
My heart which you play with!
Your rounded knees kept together.

Your gaunt cheek which you stipple
With alert satin beauty-marks;
Your pointed breasts where the morning's
Light places two pastilles.

– Stay skinny, O my little toothpick!
Keep for my ancient worship
That skeletal elegance of yours
Wherein each sex plays its part.

# Grisaille

*For Henry Céard.*

I

The rain falls in drops like cold tears.
They tinkle on the ground, funereal.

O night, smooth out the creases
In your coat of darknesses!

The day has died; in gray rays
Its murky glow is diminished.

Wrap around me, O bitter skies,
Your long dark arms; O night, promise!

No moon on this sad evening:
It has retracted its slow horns.

The street lamps in the evening
Cast sanguineous marks on the pavement.

Melancholy and boredom, grave tyrants,
Stand with impure foot on our necks;

The clock face sounds a death rattle...
It is your bell that knells, old world!

II

O Youth, why must your prism

Shatter in our hands?

Glory, that subtle incense,
Evaporates in the slightest breeze.

Goodness... a deceiving word
When rotten luck hems you in.

Virtue? The frailest wind
Defoliates this hothouse flower.

You, Beauty, a delicate pastel,[15]
Time bullies you without respite.

Hope... an immortal dream
That never materializes...

Friendship, in this false century,
Was murdered by egoism

And the least of its faults
Is being a prostitute.

As for Love, may it be cursed,
O vainest of all terms!

Love, Love, someone said it well:
You are a costly contact of epidermises.

---

[15] pastel: woad (the plant).

# Jane's Fine Vices

Jane is fagged – and superlatively so!
Her ambergris-scented epidermis, ravaged by nights,
Preserves a subtle aroma that the senses exaggerate
When the clarion of nerves groans pathologically.
Jane is fagged – and superlatively so!

Her aperitive mouth has strange kisses,
Good at heart, but pillagers of phosphorus, O brains!
When the bedroom, at evening, blazes in the orange
       reflections
Of her hair winding about its tawny skein,
Her aperitive mouth has strange kisses.

Her body makes a warm and wadded divan...
From her tired eyes descends sluggishness.
Her bosom is the white pillow where, snuggled up,
Melancholy makes her over-lively caresses languid.
Her body makes a warm and wadded divan.

On her nervous clavier with its off notes
Weeps the *lamento*[16] of hearts intoxicated by
       boredom.
For all that, the *hallali* of tracked ecstasies
Rings out gaily on bellicose nights
On her nervous clavier with its off notes.

But her love is gentle like a setting sun.

---

[16]*lamento*: a mournful, plaintive aria, used particularly in Italian opera

For those who can appreciate her, in my Jane is hidden
That dolorous charm (unfamiliar to the profane)
Of a perfume that grows stale and a flower that withers,
For her love is sweet like a setting sun.

# A Genre Painting

*For Félicien Rops.*

The master left the pestle,
For the walnut plank.
He lays out on the palette,
The rainbow he just ground.

On the dark easel glimmers
A white canvas where already
Impatient he sketches
Some raja from memory!

With satisfied step he navigates
The remarkable mess
That clutters his attic
Where his studio zigzags.

Wearing a violet beret, with a pipe
Singeing his beard, he sits
Under the skylight's wan light
Falling directly on his frames.

Knock! Knock! – "Come in!" – It's the model.
The master runs to the old chest
Where the faithful frock lies,
Of painters from the Institute.

The martyr wears a smock; he enters
Proud in his heavy sabots...
Suddenly, a waistcoat over his belly
Has made him drop his jabots,

While on his back shimmers
A coat the color of a pigeon's throat,
And he shoves his large feet
Into the slippers with tight uppers.

The white peruke with a red knot
Metamorphoses the bumpkin
Who stands awkward and frozen
In his tawdry negligee.

The master makes the poor devil sit,
Nose in a dusty book;
That mannequin must hold
That irremediable pose.

Palette on thumb, he takes his place
Behind the easel, in the window's light:
He paints, he pounces, he licks, he glazes,
And sometimes he strokes his nose,

And he spends most of the day,
Magnifying glass in hand, belaboring
His work… An Englishman on tour
Will buy it without haggling!

At which time, after a moiré varnish,
That little stereotypical scene
Becomes – original title! –
   *"A Reading in the Grimoire."*[17]

---

[17] *Grimoire*: a book of spells.

# Ex Voto

I will love no one but you anymore, just you in the
 world!
Be my compass, be my sorrow and joy.
My friends have betrayed me, I dig my heel very deep
Into their vile graves without a cry or tear.

I believe in nothing anymore but your affection.
Everything but your joyous smile is false,
Or the tear that quivers on your eyelashes, O my
 mistress!
I want no other sky than the sky of your eyes.

At your knees I place my religion, and my pride,
And my dearest hopes, and my soul in tumult
Where your love entered like a knife stab.

I want to readmit exiled candors into the bedroom...
To seal my promise, on the tapering tip
Of your breasts, I suspend my heart, – in *ex-voto!*

# Byzantine Virgins

*For George Eekhoud.*

In her impalpable peignoir
    Of black tulle,
She is surely more original
    Than virginal.

Her plaster-of-Paris body has quite
    The seductive gleams:
In the morose crepe it seems
    A pink glimmer.

Unappeased kisses
    In babbling swarms
Fly at her ravished flesh,
    Warm with desire.

She is exquisite in beauties
    And goodnesses.
But despite appearances, –
    – O, how I suffer! –

Several louis sparkled
    In her sadly blinded eyes.
Why should the oldest profession
    Appear venal to me!

Why is it that money,
    afflicting and stupid,
Should appear at the end of her
    Certain caresses?

I'm not looking for your love
        Or your humor;
Stop ruining your spine,
        Beautiful machine.

Leave me then! I want none
        Of your charms,
None of that too perfect mouth,
        That you boast of!

Without alcohol, my menu is bland:
        I have come to see
Who pays for your champagne,
        And your companions,

For your laughter, and your refrains,
        Gay and uninhibited
I have come to see some rouge,
        Lovely maiden,

Some green, some blue, some crimson
        And also some yellow!
And to inhale the aromatics
        Of your matte skin.

To note the dubious perfumes
        Of a thousand odors
Which are the incenses of your scant,
        Quiet hovel!

On the duly gilded or bronzed
        Wainscoting,

In an impetuous act,
    The body detaches

Its contours and its silhouette –
    With its vivid toilette...
And yet, obsessive equivocation!
    This corner reminds me,

With its pale and stylish world
    Standing out
Against a background of gold
    And copper,

Of the old Byzantine masterpieces
    Where, O my harlots,
The chlorotic Virgins of good Gothics
    Brilliantly glimmer!

# Absinthe Litanies

Charming philter, O you whom mothers and lovers
Fear, philter with its bitter caresses,
Absinthe, come to us in our endless boredoms!

You, the sure healer of ancient sorrows,
Cut down by sorceresses on nights of old,
Absinthe, come to us in our endless boredoms!

When your soul awakens at the bottom of our glasses,
It is a song of respite that cradles you, O marvel!
Absinthe, come to us in our endless boredoms!

You wear the tender hue of Hope,
Glaucous standard flying joyously above suffering,
Absinthe, come to us in our endless boredoms!

Your dress sparkles with the fires of emerald,
It is green like the forests where June roams,
Absinthe, come to us in our endless boredoms!

When, by sullen skies, every flame is quenched,
The sea betimes assumes your radiant complexion,
Absinthe, come to us in our endless boredoms!

In their profundity, the mystical eyes of cats conceal
Your discrete sparkle amidst the golden sands,
Absinthe, come to us in our endless boredoms!

Women have called you "a poison"... Calumny!
By you, who has died? – Grief – Be blessed!

Absinthe, come to us in our endless boredoms!

Beloved lips are tasteless beside your saliva
When our tongue writhes under your olive bite,
Absinthe, come to us in our endless boredoms!

In your insouciant breast, the sighs, the sobs,
And the remorses that slay sing with obstinate voice,
Absinthe, come to us in our endless boredoms!

Fall on my heart stunned by your smoke,
Gentle as a tear, O scented drink!
Absinthe, come to us in our endless boredoms!

Herb that makes hemlock and agaric look pale,
Sole hope of hearts gnawed on by a distressful secret,
Absinthe, come to us in our endless boredoms!

Gold and billon for people whose soul is spent,
Lamp for strong minds when the thought errs,
Absinthe, come to us in our endless boredoms!

Sister to sinister café promoters of white nights,
Nerve of the poet lost under our skies, dismal planks!
Absinthe, come to us in our endless boredoms!


ORISON

Glory and praise to you on this somber earth,
Savorous ocean where every dark rancor founders!
If ever, O immortal hypnotizer of torments,
The girl that I love should be false to her promises,

Having renounced our affections, scorned our joys,
Then, ardent beverage, come claim your victim:
I welcome your scalding, and with all my heart
I vow an unrivaled altar to you – GREEN POISON! –

# To Two Big Bizarre Eyes

Your eyes, your two beautiful eyes, your wild eyes,
Are so big that each one stubbornly tries
To find you, can you believe it?
Eyes all around your head.

Under your bangs of a griffon,
They flash like embers on an opaque night,
And they make your lips,
The sisters of strawberries, look pale!

Under their long-veiled lids,
Those eyes, candid and perverse,
Which constellate your face, –
Are they red or brown, grey or green?

Are they azure or cornflower-blue?
Who can resolve this problem?...
– They are black: the raven's wing
Looks pallid beside their velvet.

They are black, these bad actors
Where no tear is ever shed.
The devil must have fashioned this jet,
Sprinkling them with infernal soot!

Their ebony took its flight
In the forests of a powerful shore,
And their lacquer was the treasure
Of an incomparable consignment.

From what mine is this coal,
Sequined with funereal micas,
That in their good and gentle mirror
The rancor of darkness is poured?

They are sparkling gems extracted
From the sea one stormy evening;
Nights have tempered these playthings
With the most magical of stupors.

In what terrible auto-da-fé,
Was their bitumen triturated,
Or torrefied the coffee
With whose bitterness they are made?

What bold jeweler
Cut these brilliants in a somber fire,
Black stars of my skies,
Opening two dark holes in the night.

By what puff will their steel
Be powdered with bright particles?...
They are everything one could wish for:
Stars, gems, flowers, sparkles.

But for me these eyes are
Inextinguishable candles
Which my Sonnets, filled with emotion,
And my Nostalgia keep turning round.

# Madrigal of Sorts

My shame, this morning, is equals to my disgust.
Melancholic remorsefulness enters my heart.
Yesterday evening, seized by a fit of melancholy,
I stole a kiss from a woman on the street.

– Sad kiss, bitter kiss, punished kiss!
Oh! It altered me with that profane wine
Of a venal and abandoned love, and it withers
The chaste blossoming of our blessed love!...

Just until dawn, I had to endure the caresses
Of this woman who sells herself, body and mind;
She made fearsome attacks on my virtue, my languor
Was about to be re-awakened by a new call

When, deep inside me, plaintive but not spiteful,
A voice whispered: "Do not forget!"
Then the girl, as much as she tendered and multiplied
The sensual treasures of her stimulating mouth,

My heart was colder than hers, that icicle!...
She plundered my body, my unresponsive body, –
But all during this violation, my soul kept for ransom
The dear memory of you, slumbering inside me!

# The Fur

O intimate evenings of December!
One of those evenings, a red and black evening,
You draped your fur, – like a peignoir, –
Over your beautiful body with amber pallors.

A massive and heavy fur,
A fur with a subtle stench,
It muted with its wooly shape
Your lines with their stark accents.

Compared to your white, delicate flesh,
The savage pelisse possessed
The soft embraces of a kitten
And the caresses of eider down.

Marble, bronze, nacre, golden ewer,
In conquest under that fleece, –
What treasures I did glimpse gleaming there
In warm shadows, O ardent Jason!...

Weary finally by this finery,
You let the fur, tamed monster,
Fall to your feet, and standing there
You were invincible in your nudity!

Like a warrior song, the musky odor
Cast its clinking-clanking into the air,
Accompanying its clamors, in your bedroom,
With the proud hosannah of your flesh.

# Hymn

Virtue goes with wan face, lined with wrinkles.
It lowers a lifeless eye and smiles with yellow teeth...
*Your* pale face has no wrinkles, and in your ardent
glances

Something of the winged reflection of the cantharides
passes.

I know Virtue is thin. But I hate an *écorché*.
Your bosom, in its snow, has exquisite curves:
Fruits of flesh, O my hunger, for which you salivate,

Apples glorifying the espalier of Sin!

In your mind a troubling flora breaks out,
And as they are not of the richest of copses...
They are the flowers of Evil, O my dear bouquets...

Your mouth is a blossom bleeding and bathing me in
blood.

Compared to you, I disdain the insupportable pallor
And lily-innocence radiating from the face of virgins.
Your hypostasis, which Evil should light candles to,

Proves how gorgeous Vice is in full flower.

In this way I want to love you, head to foot,
With gluttonous affection, raw and unceremonious.
Chaste love is for cripples or eunuchs:

Yield to my appetencies your large and indecent
    body!

# Make-up

### I

Knowing my disgust of a libertine
For what young blood displays
Of its hematin, – one morning
You made yourself up, to please me.

You know the bizarre lodestone
And cursed attraction
That withered, desperately troubling things
Hold for me:

Buds of one evening dead on the stem,
Dewdrops at dawn without gleamings,
Stale and murderous perfumes
That my boredom lingers on, flittering.

The irremediable enemy
Of an inflexible sky's azure,
My soul, you know, my love,
Loves only what is artificial:

The *Strass* that divas embellish with,
*Tombac*, taffeta flowers,
Artificial suns: stars in heaps...
Rancors that my boredom forever fixates!

Now, knowing that I absolutely hate
The bursting joy of roses
And that the pallor of chloroses

Alone holds a certain appeal to me,

Dampening the brightness of your precious blood
By the unwholesome make-up that I adore,
Under the morbid flower of a plaster, –
Look at you and the white lilies of your flesh.

## II

Out of doors, the adorable reveille of
Of crazy springtime resounded,
Acclaiming the heated rendezvous
Of sparrows in zigzagging pursuits.

The sky blazed, immense and blue,
Making, in her bedroom,
The beads of her amber attire
Clash with the blinding sun's rays.

Unnerved by this debauchery
Of flames, beams, light shafts,
I implored the shade of gay retreats
Where dreams take shape in the mind.

I implored the darkness and its mantle
In which all things are wrapped,
When suddenly, under your pink fingers,
The thick curtain dropped.

Night, artificial and domineering,
Making brightness its subject,
Softening loud objects,
Descended like a caress.

Far from the sun's brash din
And its vulgar orgies,
You made a vermillion will-o'-the-wisp
Waver from the candle wicks.

To put some order to your make-up,
Perfumed waters, powders, oils, creams, –
Pigments that my hunger finds its nourishment in, –
Were pillaged in gallant enterprise.

### III

Half-naked, standing, with a wrist nested
In your golden chignon whence unfurled
The warm perfumes of its swell,
You smiled like Psyche.

On the marble washstand
Amidst a spate of elegant tubes,
Unguents interpreted their musical scales,
The sonorities of your palette.

Your blood flowed at the surface of your skin,
But like a flower that wilts,
Suddenly your skin had a doleful appearance
As the diaphanous *Cold cream* was applied.

*Lait d'iris, Blanc impératrice,*
*Crème Ninon,* all the white greases,
On your face, your neck, your arms,
Applied their snowy caprices.

The powder puff, in line with my wishes,
Caused a *Poudre divine* to fall:
Like diamonds on your fine skin,
And a tawny gold in your hair.

The cute little rabbit's foot,
Tinted with *Rouge végétal,*
Gave you a metallic sheen,
And a hue of feverish red peony.

With *Noir indien* rubbed under your eyes
Your pupils looked larger and more distant,
And the *Azurine* gave your eyes
An aureole of voluptuousness.

A light glaze, *Bistre* or *Sienne,*
Bronzed the edges of your lashes,
And you lined the arch of your eyebrows
With *Poudre circassienne.*

*Carmin* enlivened each earlobe
With a shade of mother of pearl,
As well as your peerless nostrils
And the dimple on your chin.

In the midst of stumped *Blues,*
A discreet brush on the temples
Muddled the fine network of your veins
Effecting a trompe-l'oeil.

Your curved nape was musk-scented
With perfumes that damn the flesh:
*Ylang, New morn hay, Frangipane,*

*Stéphanotis* and *Champacca*.

On your mouth, that glistening flower,
In this lively but unwholesome bouquet,
Soon *Pommade Raisin* was placed,
Spreading its garish shellac.

Finally a beauty mark made of velvet,
At the corner of one eye fixing me
Like an assassin, was put into place...
And you raised the heavy curtains.

### IV

The sun immediately, despotically!
Rushes into the room,
Chasing with an incongruous flame
The charming chorus of shadows.

In its light, which enhances
Your delicate make-up,
You appeared to me in the total brilliance
Of your false flower's florescence.

Beautiful for the novel embellishments
That double your seduction,
You sounded, by my troubled senses,
The *mort* of voluptuousness.

Mad with desire, I embraced you,
Planting ardent kisses on your head,
Your face, your neck, your teeth,
Wherever my lust carried me.

On your eyes, animal enchantresses,
On your nostrils with its troubling wing,
On your tobacco-brown nape whither flew
My desire, amidst the scents.

On your ear, a sea shell,
Where I whispered my rude confessions...
When, all of a sudden, my spirited kisses
Had removed all your make-up!

V

Sulky, with quarrelsome eyes, looking out
From under a thick veil of hair,
You disappeared behind your washstand,
To revive your pallors.

Stop your hasty hand, love:
Drop your pastes, unguents,
And extravagant pastels...
Even if I adore you made-up!

Your palette is just a decoy
Whose colors are too ephemeral,
My love has nimble fingers:
Let *it* be the painter of your skin!

More fertile in cunning than you are,
To animate your pallid traits,
It will take my fondness for make-up
And your despair of *ceruses*.

My nibbles will know how to hollow
Rosy dimples into your flesh;
Disdainful of morose shellacs
Come empurple yourself with my kisses.

My teeth, on our nights of conquest,
Will place their beauty marks.
My fingernails, without complacency,
Will be equal to your depilatory.

My solicitude will blue your eyes
Than pencils or stones could even better,
And our vigils, on your eyelids,
Will sew mourning into the borders...

Your make-up is a vain daubing,
It cannot withstand the tears.
My burning love is all you need
To make you up for years!

# Other Books by the Publisher

*Fanchette's Pretty Little Foot* by Restif de La Bretonne

*Je M'Accuse...* by Léon Bloy

*My Hospitals & My Prisons* by Paul Verlaine

*Salvation Through the Jews* by Léon Bloy

*Words of a Demolitions Contractor* by Léon Bloy

*Cellulely* by Paul Verlaine

*Ecclesiastical Laurels* by Jacques Rochette de la Morlière

*Flowers of Bitumen* by Émile Goudeau

*Songs for Her & Odes in Her Honor* by Paul Verlaine

*On Huysmans' Tomb* by Léon Bloy

*Ten Years a Bohemian* by Émile Goudeau

*The Soul of Napoleon* by Léon Bloy

*Blood of the Poor* by Léon Bloy

*Joan of Arc and Germany* by Léon Bloy

*A Platonic Love* by Paul Alexis

*The Revealer of the Globe: Christopher Columbus & His Future Beatification (Part One)* by Léon Bloy

*An Immodest Proposal* by Dr. Helmut Schleppend

*The Pornographer* by Restif de La Bretonne

*Style (Theory and History)* by Ernest Hello

*On the Threshold of the Apocalypse: 1913-1915* by Léon Bloy

*She Who Weeps (Our Lady of La Salette)* by Léon Bloy

*The Sylph* by Claude Prosper Jolyot de Crébillon (*fils*)

*Voyage in France by a Frenchman* by Paul Verlaine

*Ourigan, Oregon* by William Clark, Richard Robinson, and anonymous

*Drowning* by Yu Dafu

*Cull of April* by Francis Vielé-Griffin

*The Misfortune of Monsieur Fraque* by Paul Alexis

*Fêtes Galantes & Songs Without Words* by Paul Verlaine

*Joys* by Francis Vielé-Griffin

*The Son of Louis XVI* by Léon Bloy

*Septentrion* by Jean Raspail

*The Resurrection of Villiers de l'Isle-Adam* by Léon Bloy

*Poems Saturnian* by Paul Verlaine

*The Biography of Léon Bloy: Memories of a Friend* by René Martineau

*Fredegund, France: A Book of Poetry* by Richard Robinson

*The Good Song* by Paul Verlaine

*Swans* by Francis Vielé-Griffin

*Constantinople and Byzantium* by Léon Bloy

*Enamels and Cameos* by Théophile Gautier

*Four Years of Captivity in Cochons-sur-Marne: 1900-1904* by Léon Bloy

*Dark Minerva: Prolegomena: The Moral Construction of Dante's Divine Comedy* by Giovanni Pascoli

*What is Fascism: Discourses and Polemics* by Giovanni Gentile

*The Desperate Man* by Léon Bloy

*Meditations of a Solitary in 1916* by Léon Bloy

*The Ride of Yeldis & Other Poems* by Francis Vielé-Griffin

*Silvie & The Chimeras* by Gérard de Nerval

*Italian Nationalism* by Enrico Corradini

*A Silver-Grey Death* and *Drowning* by Yu Dafu

*Doctrines of Hatred, Part I: Anti-Semitism* by Anatole Leroy-Beaulieu

www.ingramcontent.com/pod-product-compliance
Lightning Source LLC
LaVergne TN
LVHW040108080526
838202LV00045B/3818